Loss and Grief Counseling Skills

the practical wording of therapeutic statements and processes

Daniel Keeran, MSW

Copyright © 2010 by Daniel Keeran, MSW

All rights reserved. No part of this book may be used or reproduced in any manner whatsoever without specific written permission from the author except in the case of brief quotations in reviews for inclusion in a magazine, newspaper, or broadcast.

ISBN 1453644393

EAN-13 9781453644393

Library of Congress Control Number: 2010909087

Library Cataloguing in Publication Data

Keeran, Daniel M., 1947-
    Loss and grief counseling skills: the practical wording of therapeutic statements and processes/ Daniel Keeran.

Includes index.
ISBN 978-1-4536443-9-3

1. Grief counseling. 2. Mental health counseling. I. Title.

| BF727.3.L66 K45 2010 | 155.9 | 2010909087 |

Printed in the United States of America.

Author contact:
collegemhc@gmail.com

Dedicated to

Jennie, Phoebe, and Seth

Table of Contents

Introduction to Loss and Grief	7
Types of Losses	8
Emotions of Grief	13
Goals of Grief Counseling	14
Interventions for Emotions of Grief	16
Unfinished Business of Grief	29
Letting Go of Expectations of Parental Caring	31
Protection Block	32
Grieving Loss of Parental Caring	32
Behaviour Decisions in Grief Counseling	35
Interventions to Engage Grieving	38
Working with Behaviour Decisions	41
Working with Unfinished Business	42
The Empty Chair Technique	43
Pace of the Session	48
Opening the Session	48
Demonstration of Grief Counseling	49

Index	53
About the Author	55

This discussion of loss and grief counseling is a continuation of therapeutic interventions and a preparation for conflict resolution discussed in detail in the training manual *Effective Counseling Skills: the practical wording of therapeutic statements and processes* available through major bookstores and Amazon here at http://www.amazon.com/Effective-Counseling-Skills-therapeutic-statements/dp/1442177993 The text is written in an informal style from the actual class discussion transcript and includes occasional student comments. The *Grief Counseling Theory and Skills* course is available at http://www.collegemhc.com

In terms of significant unresolved conflicts and losses, every conflict is a loss because conflict creates distance in relationships. We will begin now to discuss losses, and then later in the above-mentioned training manual that the reader is encouraged to read, we will discuss more about conflicts, specifically how to work with the client, and how to deal with conflicts in his relationships, past and present.

INTRODUCTION TO LOSS AND GRIEF

First of all we want to review the types of loss that people experience, the goals of grief counseling, painful feelings around loss and grief, the unfinished business of loss, and the behaviour decisions of grief, and then we'll look at some therapeutic interventions.

Loss is part of the human condition. There's no way we can avoid loss. It's something we experience from the time we're born to the time we die. We experience losses every step of the way throughout our lives, such as the loss of a job, loss of health, and loss of relationships through a break up or through death, to name a few.

Because we are bound by time, every passing moment is a loss, but not every loss involves grief. We need to distinguish between loss and grief. Loss is a word that refers to an event in which something that we had or were attached to was lost. It can also refer to something that we needed or wished for, but never had. So loss doesn't necessarily have to do with attachment or having had something that was lost. There's a saying that you can't lose something that you've never had, but I disagree with that. I think you can have an experience of loss of something that you needed but never had.

Parental caring is a good example. If I never got the caring I needed from my father, that was a loss, even if I never had it in the first place. So an unmet need itself could be considered a loss.

Abraham Maslow identified a hierarchy of needs that we have at different stages of our lives as we develop. And the primary need that we're working with, with many clients, is the need for closeness and caring. Everybody needs that. Every child needs and deserves that as she grows up. That's a primary loss that we're helping the clients to grieve. Loss is referring to the event, grief is the emotional reaction to the event.

TYPES OF LOSSES

Let's make a list of types of losses that we experience and which we're going to be wanting to identify later with our clients as we do the assessment and work with them in the counseling relationship. The list will be in the order that we experience them from our birth to our death.

First of all, how is birth a loss? It's a loss of the safe, secure environment that we were in. Our needs for warmth, and nourishment were met, and we were cushioned by that water around us so we didn't have to worry about being jolted, jarred, and bumped so much. So when a child is born it cries to have its needs met. It didn't have to cry before, but at birth now it has to cry to get itself changed, to get fed, to get warm, to get put to bed. There's quite a radical change that comes with birth. Who else loses when there's a birth? The mother.

How is that a loss for Mom?

Student comment: I'm thinking about my daughter. I really enjoyed being pregnant with her. Lying in bed at night and feeling the baby move was such a wonderful feeling that it's hard to explain it. She was born at seven in the evening and the next day when the doctor came in to make his rounds, I was weeping. I explained to him that I was happy she was born and that she was there, but even now I get choked when I think about this. It was like she had been mine, my own, and now I had to share her with everybody. And all of a sudden she was out in the world, and there were other people standing over her and being around her all the time. It was just like she wasn't mine any more. And I really wept over that for about two or three days after. It took a long time. And the doctor couldn't understand it. He said, "You're the first patient I've had who has said that." He said, "Everybody's so glad the baby is out." I really missed her after that. I had to put my arms around her to hold her.

That's a loss for a Mom and for Dad, especially with the first born. It's a loss of a certain type of relationship between the parents because now there's a third individual. They're no longer two, now they're three. And the special one-on-one relationship that was there before has really changed. The attention goes to this demanding entity constantly needing to be changed and fed and so on. And sometimes marriages find that the loss of what they had previously is so difficult to accept that the marriage is strained or does not survive. Especially if, for example, the father married mother to get caring needs met, and now he's no longer getting that caring because the attention is being diverted to someone else. He may try to get it from somewhere else. And so relationships can break down with a birth.

What would be the next loss for the baby as it's growing up? Weaning. Some mothers find that to be a loss as well. She doesn't want to let go. I've heard of mothers nursing babies until they're six or seven years old.

I haven't seen evidence that it has any detrimental affect for the child or the mother. So I wouldn't say that it's healthy or unhealthy to hang on to that. It depends on what the child's experience is. I haven't heard anyone report what he considered abusive to him.

Having a child is a continuous experience of loss because from day one the dependency of the child on the mother is constantly declining. Certainly there is a loss of independence. Many mothers and many fathers experience that loss of freedom and independence because they feel tied to the responsibility of raising the child. There is the loss of freedom with parental responsibility, but then when the child is gone one feels the loss of the child and the emptiness that goes with it.

Then we can identify infertility or not having a child or children as a loss. You can take it as gain because then you have a baby and then the baby has babies, then all the way around it can be more of a gain than a loss. This introduces the idea of reconstruction of one's life following a loss and perhaps reframing loss or identifying the gain within the loss. So the same experience can have two sides. It can be the gain aspect and the loss aspects.

When the child has his own mobility after being weaned or he begins to walk there's the loss of having to carry the child around. Any developmental change is a loss because the child no longer is attended in the same way. Because it can walk, it has to accept a little bit more responsibility for itself and at the same time has to be watched more. Toilet training is a loss. So what we are seeing is that every change is loss and gain.

What comes after that for a child? Going to school. Leaving home, passing from one grade to the next. What are some more along the way there? Then there is loss of friends. Young families are highly mobile, and the child's friends may be members of young families that move away, or the child's family may move.

Maybe for the child there is a loss of staying in the home environment all the time. Now he's having to go out and interact in the school environment. Loss of the safety and security of home can be scary. The question we wonder is how did the client adjust to this early separation kind of loss.

A mother going back to work could be a loss maybe being replaced by a babysitter or a nanny or not being home when the child returns from school and having to be home alone.

A major loss can happen with the arrival of a sibling. Now there is someone there to compete for the special attention that the child received. In my own family that's the basis of the rivalry. My oldest is a girl who has said at times that when her brother was born "he took my life away". So it's a very real loss and it sets up a rivalry of unresolved grief and conflict that can stay all through adult years. What comes after that?

Puberty, the loss of early childhood is a loss. First sexual experiences even before puberty may constitute a loss of a sense of innocence for a child.

When the child starts dating, that can be a loss for parents because her attention and affection are directed toward someone else. And for some young people maybe dating is a loss because it represents growing up and becoming more separate from the nuclear family. For this reason a child may resist or be frightened by dating.

The same thing happens to people who have to go to work too early in life, loss of childhood. Then there is graduation from school and leaving home with loss of security for the child and empty nest for the parent.

Then becoming attached to a mate, they experience the loss of single life, of freedom. When people cry at their weddings, they may be grieving the loss of their single life. It's a huge step to make such vows to enter into a life-long relationship.

What comes after marriage? You lose your single friends. At least that happens to a lot of people. Then come children or divorce, another enormous loss that can take years to recover from and can affect future relationships and the children as well.

By now, perhaps someone close has died, deaths of grandparents. And then your parents die, and you lose your whole frame of reference. I am who I am because I know my parents live over there in Marion, Ohio. And when they die, it's as if I'm not from Ohio any more. My parents haven't died yet, but I wonder: where will I go? I won't go back to Ohio.

One may experience the loss of closeness with family members after the parents die. All the other relatives are on their own, unless you reach out. The parents had connected everyone and arranged reunions. There's a loss of family ties.

Maybe there is unemployment, illness, retirement. Somewhere around middle age there is a loss of youth. The body starts to go down, and there's a loss of energy. You could lose your teeth, possible loss of virility, going through menopause, and so on.

Then if you give up smoking or drinking, there can be the loss of habits or addictions. One must face the loss of a thing to experience the gain. Otherwise, one will struggle more to let go of the addiction.

There are also losses that occur on a societal level. It seems to me that there's a loss of innocence now with environmental awareness. We can't go on doing what we are doing. We have lost the belief in unending resources. We don't have that kind of freedom anymore. We have to watch ourselves. That's a loss of ignorance, and you can also think of it as a loss of innocence.

Moving from one town to another can be a major loss. For some people who move from one culture to another there is also a loss of culture. Other losses could be suicides or homicides, which may be very significant losses.

Loss of property, financial loss, bankruptcy, and adoption are losses. We may have been adopted ourselves or perhaps had to give up a child for adoption as a birth parent. Then comes aging, loss of our faculties, possibly terminal illness, facing our own death.

Some of the other losses that we have
loss of the family of origin by going into fc
loss of puppy love, loss of the first partr
death, miscarriage or abortion.

The reason we have reviewed the ty
an awareness of how pervasive and varic
is one's life. In order for us, and our client, to live in a ...
way, we need to allow ourselves to accept the normality of our
losses and their painful aspects as well as the process of healing
and progress.

EMOTIONS OF GRIEF

It's important to point out that the intensity of our grief varies according to the type of loss, and the degree of emotional bonding to what was lost. The specific painful feeling may vary according to the type of loss.

Think of fear, anger, guilt, sadness, emptiness, low self-worth, and despair. These are the seven primary painful feelings. Which feeling do you think stands out with suicide of a loved one? What do the surviving family members feel? Guilt stands out above the others. You can feel all the other emotions strongly but guilt is primary because it's a feeling that the client could have said something or should have observed something.

What about the empty nest? When the last child leaves home? Emptiness. What about adoption? What does the adopted person feel deep down? Low self-worth. What about a crib death? Guilt. What about bankruptcy? Despair, low self-worth. People kill themselves because their worth is attached to their financial resources, and when they've lost that then their own worth is gone. What's the point of living if you have no worth?

What about retirement? What would be a primary feeling there? Emptiness. Maybe you put all your energy, your whole self, into your work. All your eggs have been in that basket, and retired and it's all gone. People tend to identify ...es with their work role, and if that's a really strong role ...t ends, they may not know who they are anymore. The ...llenge is to be resilient, flexible, and adaptable.

one loss can be multiple losses

One loss often results in multiple loss. For example, I have a client who had a brain tumor about eight years ago. She underwent surgery, and as a result she lost her job, and she lost her husband who couldn't cope with her resulting disability. She had to go into a group home so she lost her independence, and she had never had any children so the prospect of having children was lost. She had an impaired memory, impaired vision, impaired speech, and had to use a walker to get around. She had multiple physical losses and the losses of roles and relationships.

A mother died when my client was 10 years old, and this loss left her afraid to be close to her own daughters, so she lost the emotional bond that could have been. When she worked through the death of her mother and grieved what she lost in closeness with her children, she was able to reclaim the relationship with her daughters.

Parenting is another example. When your children leave home, you not only lose them but you lose the role of being a parent. And that kind of ripple effect may be true of a number of types of losses.

GOALS OF GRIEF COUNSELING

The primary goal of grief counseling is to deal with the seven most painful feelings; everything else is a derivative of them. Every other painful feeling can be related to those. For example, anger is at the root of resentment and frustration, fear is the source of anxiety and insecurity, and emptiness gives rise to abandonment and loneliness. Shame is a combination of fear and guilt. It's a fear about what other people may think if they knew.

There are three goals in grief counseling. The first and fundamental goal is to identify and experience the range and intensity of painful feelings that make up grief. We're going to help the client to identify the feelings cognitively, and then to experience the full range from fear to despair as well as the intensity of the painful feelings related to his loss, or losses.

The second goal is to identify changes or maladaptive behaviour decisions which are related to the loss. This goal is very important in cases of complicated loss, which occurs when the painful feelings have not been dealt with in a healthy way. Instead of being expressed and shared, they've been defended against and protected, resulting in unhealthy or maladapted behaviours. By maladaptive we mean ineffective or unworkable or unhealthy behaviour decisions. When we see these behaviours continuing over years, over a long period of time, then we're seeing this as a complicated bereavement experience of our client.

"Decisions" is an interesting word because the behaviour choices, or ways of coping with the pain, are often done unintentionally or unconsciously, but they are decisions nonetheless. A person can re-decide, can make different decisions about that pain and how to cope with it, how to deal with it.

The third goal of grief counseling is to complete unfinished business, and to say goodbye in order to say hello. It's difficult to say hello to new life experiences until we say goodbye to old painful ones, and by goodbye we mean letting go. Saying goodbye, and letting go, and learning acceptance, which is a commonly used term, all mean the same thing.

Saying goodbye really encompasses all three objectives for grief counseling. A person hasn't completely grieved, or said goodbye, or let go, until he has worked through the pain, identified and changed the behaviour decisions, and finished his unfinished business.

You can see that these goals correspond to the counseling process as we've been discussing it. It's simply a reiteration of what we've been talking about. As we're discussing loss and grief, I'd like for you to be thinking about your own losses. These could be deaths of loved ones, break-up of relationships, loss of parental caring and relationships are the major ones, the most difficult ones.

Once you've identified a loss and the person can express the sadness, how often do you go back to that loss? Maybe you think a person could experience those feelings surrounding a loss indefinitely just by putting himself back in that place again. How do you know when enough is enough?

There are two different views. The cognitive school says you don't really get rid of the pain, you just know all about it. You become so familiar with it that it no longer has power over you. And the only way to know all about it is to experience it. There's no other way. So there is a point at which cognitive therapy has to include grieving, otherwise there's no true knowledge of the pain.

The other school of thought which is represented, for example, by people who use psychodrama a lot, is that when you express the pain it's possible to release it, and to purge yourself of it. It may take a long time for that catharsis to be complete, but eventually the pain will be completely gone.

I tend to think it's a combination of both. There is a catharsis effect, and some of the pain is released, but then there is also the cognitive aspect of knowing about the intensity of the pain, that takes the power away from it. I'm no longer frightened of the pain. I know about it and I've accepted it as mine, and as okay. I have embraced the pain.

INTERVENTIONS FOR THE EMOTIONS OF GRIEF

Now let's go on to looking at the painful feelings. The first goal of grief counseling is to identify and experience the range and intensity of painful feelings. It's going to be important for us to review these feelings and to suggest some therapeutic interventions for working with the grieving person. We also need to realize what the fear of painful feelings is about.

Imagine a successful executive of a corporation who has never experienced any tragedy in his life, any major loss. He has a wife and three kids and he gets a phone call that one of his children, a six or seven year old child, has just been hit by a truck and killed in front of the house. The child came home from school and crossed the road in front of a gravel truck coming from a nearby construction site, and was killed. Now this man has a lot of responsibility to provide for his family and to keep his company going, and since he has experienced a tragic loss he goes for counseling. It's very difficult for him to engage his pain, because he's afraid of what?

He's afraid of falling apart and of not being able to get on with all of the things he has to do. He needs to maintain the image of the corporate person. And he's been working on being able to do this for many years and to continue with his heavy responsibilities. So not having experienced intense grief before, he doesn't know that it's not going to cause him to fall apart.

In fact he doesn't realize that if he doesn't allow himself to grieve, then he's going to fall apart. It's going to be just the opposite of what he's afraid of. So we need to help that person get past the fear, and the way to do that is to encourage him to talk about the fear, to validate the fear, to reflect how scary it may be, and then invite him just to say a little bit about it.

fear

I find this is a very effective approach when working with the very blocked, resistant client: invite him to say *just a little bit* about the *little bit of fear* that he *may* have. And once he feels supported with that, then he can go on to another painful feeling.

A gradual approach to the feared object is fundamental to working with fear. Remember that whenever there is fear, there is resistance, defenses. So it is important to go slowly, invite the person to say what the fear is about and after he has disclosed, ask him what it was like to talk about that. Then invite him to say a little more. Whenever, there is disclosure of difficult, painful experience, be sure to process the process by saying, "What was it like talking about that? Is it OK?" This allows the client to control the pace and amount of disclosure and to validate the process and to maintain his sense of safety.

Sometimes the fear is about feeling so much of the pain, he will become depressed or so sad that he will never stop crying. So we can say, "I wonder if you are afraid that if you start crying you may never stop, and you will fill the whole world with your tears." This can free up the sadness, and he will discover that the crying does end and he survived it. This will help the healing, and life will be easier and less sad.

anger

Some grieving people find it easier to access anger than their sadness. They'll use their anger to defend against their sadness. They feel strong with anger but weak and vulnerable with sadness. Generally the person who finds it easier to access anger in grief has an aggressive personality. They are usually outspoken, direct, and opinionated.

In working with the very angry, grieving client, we can validate that anger for as long as he needs it to be validated. Draw it out and encourage him to express it, entitle him to that anger.

If we're able to validate or support a person's anger, what feeling comes next? The sadness will come out more easily if the anger has been properly supported. Now with the passive individual, who accesses sadness more easily, we need to help him express the anger. The passive individual feels guilty about anger and is afraid of its destructiveness. So to reach for anger we can use the word "cheated," or another word that the person feels safer with.

So we can say, "I wonder if you feel a little cheated? Your husband has died, you expected you'd be able to retire together, you were looking forward to that. And now he's gone. I wonder if you feel just a little bit cheated about that?" And sometimes what I find is that if I minimize a feeling and use the word cheated with that individual, she'll maximize and say, "Yes, I feel really cheated." And I'll say, "Go on and say more about being cheated." In fact she is talking about her anger, but she is just not using that word.

Try to find words that don't offend the client or that don't trigger the guilt or fear around anger. Try to use other approaches and other words. Here are some other approaches.

You can say things like, "What are some 'why' questions? If you were to ask 'why' questions about the death of your father, or the death or your child, what would they be?"

What are some of those 'why' questions? Why did you die? Why him? Why did he leave me? Why not me? Why did God let this happen? Often the anger is directed at God. So then I'll say, "What's the feeling that goes with that why question? Fear, anger, guilt, sadness, emptiness?"

If it was a child the client may ask why a child died. Why not an older person? Why not someone who'd lived a full life? Why a child? Anger is what goes with that question: the outrage, the sense of injustice, the unfairness. Sometimes your client will come up with anger. Then you can invite him to say more about the anger. And you can validate it, support it.

Another thing we can do is say, "Talk about the lost hopes and dreams." Lost hopes and dreams are about being cheated because those hopes and dreams can't be fulfilled now that this death and this loss has occurred. There's a sense of feeling cheated about that. Another thing I may do to draw anger is to design a statement for my client to repeat. I may design a why question or a blaming statement.

For example in the case of an abusive parent, in working with loss of parental caring and closeness, I may suggest the statement, "You didn't care about anyone but yourself. You didn't care about me, all you cared about was the bottle." Try on that statement. I may say it without any affect in my voice.

You can tailor a statement, invite your client to repeat it, and then reach for a feeling. "What's it like saying that? Does that fit? What feelings come up when you say that? What choice words do you have for this man?" Go for choice words or strong words, if your client has them in his vocabulary. For the type of client that has choice words available to him, ask him what some choice words may be. The passive client may not have choice words in his vocabulary. Some of these words could possibly be very coarse and powerful.

We are facilitating the expression of emotion through name-calling, I'm talking here about the client who has been severely abused, mistreated. We need to have a way to vent that anger in a therapeutic setting, not face to face with the abuser. So you don't really want to escalate it but you want to allow this person to feel that it's okay to feel angry.

Sometimes anger is directed toward the counselor as a defense. When a client becomes very resistant and begins to struggle with the counselor, we can say, "So I wonder if hanging on to the struggle is a way of not getting on with your healing." When he acknowledges this, direct him, "Now talk about what's behind the struggle, talk about what's hard to talk about, what's hard to face."

sadness

When I'm starting to bring out anger and sadness with a client, I may also say, "I wonder if you're using that anger to defend against another feeling." Or "I wonder if that anger is easier than the sadness." Or if a client identifies both anger and sadness I'll say, "Which of those two feelings is easier for you to express?"

She may have identified anger as a primary feeling, and I may reach for a little sadness. She may have owned a little sadness, and then I would say, "Which one is easier for you to feel?" And whichever one she chooses I'll invite her to talk about the opposite one because it's the one she doesn't want to talk about that needs to be worked through. The key to a person's progress is to invite him to explore and integrate whatever is most difficult.

Other ways to get to sadness is to say the following:

"Say his name." The name of the loved one may be loaded with sadness and remains unspoken until you invite it.

"Talk about a happy memory." The happy memory brings up a sense of loss and sadness.

"Talk about the last time you saw him." The last memory may be of the death or of regrets and sadness about this.

"What do you see as your talk? It's as if you are looking at something." Tapping into mental images may be associated with sadness because the past is being re-lived in the present.

"You will never see his face again." The realization about the finality of the death is often very sad but true.

"Have you said good-bye to him?" This brings up sadness about the finality of the loss and can be key to letting go.

While observing the client's emotional response, take note of keywords and phrases immediately preceding the sadness, then repeat these words at an opportune time to facilitate grief. For example, a client grieves when describing how her son was killed by a "power truck." Later, I simply said, "There was a power truck," and the client cried.

Remember to always process the process after a client has finished crying, by saying, "What's its like talking about this and feeling these things? Is it OK to cry?" And if she says it hurts so much say, "It's normal to feel that with what you've been through. You loved him."

guilt

Guilt is one of the primary reasons that people develop very maladaptive behaviours. A person who feels very guilty doesn't believe that he deserves happiness, and so what does he think he think he deserves? Punishment.

Punishment goes with guilt, so I may want to explore with the person how much guilt he feels? Maybe a little bit, a lot? This is the same technique I may use exploring any feeling. How much anger do you feel? A little bit, a lot, a medium amount? I want to gauge how much of that feeling they are aware of inside.

If they feel a lot of guilt, or they identify a feeling of guilt I'm going to say, "I wonder if you're aware of how you may be punishing yourself."

And then I'll say what some people do. "Sometimes when people feel guilty they won't let themselves be happy, they'll be depressed, they'll be stuck in their life. They won't let themselves get on with their life. They won't let themselves experience enjoyment, they won't let themselves be close to people, they won't let themselves really welcome the challenges and opportunities that life has to offer. And I wonder if you're aware of how you may be punishing yourself in some small way?"

A helpful approach is to use exaggeration: "I wonder if you will give yourself a life sentence." When the client considers this, they have a chance to realize what he may have done and decide to let go of the self-punishment. "What will you do differently? Can you let go of that?" and "What would (your loved one) say?"

use of minimizing and exaggeration

So again use that minimizing technique, because it's easier for people to think of small ways sometimes and then that opens up other areas of awareness. So a person will choose and then I'll say, "I wonder if you're going to give yourself a life sentence?" That's making use of exaggeration. In other words, take that metaphor to its ultimate conclusion, or to it's extreme, which could be something like a life sentence of punishment by means of depression.

For example, I had a client who lived a rebellious life, and then his mother suddenly died of a heart attack. He blamed himself for his mother's death and he became chronically depressed after that for a number of years. When I saw him in treatment I explored the guilt with him, and I said, "I wonder how you may punish yourself? I wonder if maybe depression is a way you may do that?" And he acknowledged it. And he went on saying that he didn't deserve to be happy. He felt that his life style was a cause of his mother's death. And so I said, "I wonder if you're going to give yourself a life sentence?" And he stopped and the wheels were turning and he made a new decision. He pulled back from the guilt.

With the extreme conclusion or exaggeration intervention, a person will pull back from the exaggerated possibility. He'll say, "No, I'm not going to take it to that extent." This client started making real changes, real improvements in his direction. When people feel really guilty, they won't allow themselves to get on with their grieving. They'll remain stuck in it, and that's their unconscious form of punishment.

hanging on or letting go

Sometimes people won't let themselves work through their sadness and their anger, or other painful feelings, because hanging on to the guilt is a way of hanging on to the person who died. Sometimes I'll put it to a client that way. I'll say, "I wonder if hanging on to that guilt may be a way of hanging on to Mom?" And some times they don't realize it, they haven't thought of it in those terms. When you put it that way it helps them to decide not to hang on.

I've heard clients say that: "I don't want to hang on any more." That implies letting go of the guilt. You can use that with anger: "I wonder if hanging on to that anger is a way of hanging on to the man you divorced? Hanging on to the fight may be a way of hanging on to your ex-husband. Hanging on to the fight may be a way of hanging on to Dad."

You can move people forward by saying, "It's not easy to let go. It's not something you need to hurry." What you often hear is, "How do you let go?" and I say, "By doing exactly what you're doing today. Talking about your feelings, putting it into words, by doing exactly what you're doing and I encourage you to keep doing that. What's it like doing that today, talking about your pain?" And they'll say, "It's tough."

I mentioned earlier that some people use anger to cover sadness and others use sadness to cover anger. So sadness is not necessarily the core feeling, although often for the person who's very angry, it's important for him to get to his sadness.

For the person who's very sad, especially if he appears to be stuck in sadness over a long period of time, weeks, months, or maybe years, maybe it's because it's because he hasn't dealt with the anger, or he hasn't dealt with the guilt, or both.

emptiness

So then we come to emptiness. Emptiness is something a person may feel constantly. But sometimes a person will fill the emptiness, or attempt to fill that empty feeling or that void with the other painful feelings. It's easier to feel anger than that agonizing emptiness or that sense of the void, that abandonment, that loneliness.

Sometimes, early on in grief counseling, that person may identify feeling empty, and the way I may work with that is to say, "What goes into that emptiness? Would it be empty sad, empty angry, empty frightened, empty guilty, empty what?" I'll associate another feeling with the emptiness.

And I may work with the emptiness on its own, and just invite the person to talk about the emptiness. She may talk about a loved one she lost, who had been in her life at the dinner table, or in bed beside her if it's a partner, a spouse. The spouse came to the door at the same time on schedule for so many years, and now that person is gone and so there are empty spaces at the table, in the bedroom, at the door.

When a child dies there is tremendous emptiness because that child has occupied so much of the parents' time, and has contributed so much to the noise level. The child leaves a deafening silence that's very agonizing. We need to help a person identify what the emptiness is about and then validate that.

Now the emptiness may become more apparent to a person as she gets support and is able to put these other painful feelings, the anger or sadness, into words. As she's letting go of that anger or sadness, the emptiness may still be there and it may be even more obvious to the person. And most especially, I find that clients report feeling empty when I invite them to talk about letting go or saying goodbye to the loved one.

For example, I sometimes use the empty chair to invite a person to talk to a loved one about saying goodbye, and I then explore the feelings that he's left with. I say, "What's it like, what are you feeling inside as you say goodbye and as you talk about saying goodbye to your father or your child? What feelings come up? Fear, anger, guilt, emptiness, despair?" And nine times out of ten they choose emptiness because that's what's left if you're going to say goodbye to somebody.

Now if a person has done a fair amount of grieving, I'll work with that emptiness in a therapeutic way by saying, "Maybe you're at a kind of crossroads in your grief. You can either fill that emptiness with the old pain, your old ways of being stuck and not getting on with your life, not letting yourself be close to other people, or you can begin to fill that emptiness with the challenges that life has to offer, taking risks to get close, allowing yourself to enjoy pleasurable experiences in life. Which way do you think you'll go on this crossroad?"

That's a cognitive technique that allows clients to make a conscious decision about what they're going to do or which way they're going to go. This is transition toward reconstruction of life and saying hello to new people and experiences.

how long is grief?

What kind of a time frame are we looking at? I mean you can't say, "It's been three months, it's time to do something." But roughly, how long do people need to grieve? It really depends. If you lose a child you may grieve for years. To assess that, we're looking at the individual's ability to function. Is this person able to go back to work, able to get on with the important aspects of his life? Or is he still doing things that are getting in the way of family, social relationships and work?

Has there been some grief that appears to be getting in the way? Depending upon the type of loss, such as the loss of a family member, we may expect a person to grieve intensely. If he was emotionally bonded to someone, he may grieve intensely for maybe a year. He may be able to get back to work after a month but the pain of that grief may hang on for considerable time, even for years to come.

seeing the hidden loss

If there was emotional distance, a loss of bonding, or if the lost person was experienced as angry, the grief may be buried and be more about the loss of closeness when the person was alive or prior to the loss.

A woman married a man who disclosed to her after two or three years of marriage that he was homosexual, and then he ended the relationship. She didn't appear to go through any grieving process at all when it actually ended. She went back to work the next day and two months later she met another man. She got married and had kids, and I'm not aware of her going through much grief. Why? Because the marriage was the loss not the ending of the marriage. She grieved when she first learned he was gay. She was angry, sad; felt guilt, low self-worth, emptiness.

Grief will only be experienced as an intense kind of experience if there's been bonding. If there hasn't been significant emotional bonding, it's not as much of a loss. If he was homosexual it's understandable that there may not have been much intimacy, or closeness, or bonding. It may have been some other kind of relationship, more like a brother and sister rather than husband and wife. So it has to do with how much is invested.

A woman came up to me after a talk I had given and said that when her mother died she didn't grieve. And she wanted to know why, because other people grieve. She wondered why she wasn't upset. I asked her, "Were you close to your mother?" and she said "No." She had never been close all those years. And I said, "I wonder what feelings come up inside you when you think about all those years of not being close to your mother?" That's when the tears welled up in her eyes. That's what her grief was about. It wasn't about her mother's death. It was about the loss of closeness during her lifetime.

low self-worth

A person may feel low self-worth, especially if he is experiencing feelings of guilt, because when a person feels very guilty he doesn't feel worthwhile, he doesn't feel he deserves to go on living.

A person may also experience low self-worth if he comes from a dysfunctional family and now has experienced a tragic death of a loved one. He may feel as though he didn't really deserve to have that person be alive for him.

Low self-worth sometimes happens when people bargain, for example with God, over the life of the person who died. So you may hear about a person saying, "I'm really the one who should die. Don't let that child die. Take me, God." So in that kind of bargaining the implied message is, "I'm not as worthwhile as the child." A person may then become very depressed, and isolate or deprive himself of enjoyment in life because he doesn't feel worthwhile or deserving.

In cases of sexual abuse, low self-worth is connected to shame or to feeling dirty. What do you do with something if it's dirty or worthless? You throw it away. That's another kind of loss that we haven't yet talked about. Sexual abuse and assault is a very significant loss. Feeling dirty or feeling shame is closely related to that and leads to self-abuse by choosing unhealthy relationships and lifestyle or behaviours that distance from others, such as obesity or aggression.

despair

Despair and hopelessness are the sum total of these other painful feelings, and as a person is engaging in the grief process and getting support and validation, often that despair will diminish. The despair may appear early on along with fear, but as the safety of the counseling relationship increases and the therapeutic alliance improves, despair sometimes diminishes along with the fear.

Despair often goes with confusion. A person may have a lot of painful feelings inside that he hasn't identified, especially early in the grief process. He feels despair because he has the intensity of all that pain but he hasn't been able to sort it out. So as you work with him throughout the process and identify the distinct feelings and help him work through them, the confusion and the despair diminish.

prior loss affecting a current loss

If a person has suffered significant losses throughout her lifetime, is the coping process easier for her? It depends on how she has dealt with those previous losses. If she has coped with her previous losses in an unhealthy way by burying feelings, or by dumping feelings, or by distancing herself from others, that can become a pattern.

For example, some people won't say goodbye. They'll just leave and you'll wonder where they went. And it may be that that's related to their style of hanging on or their style of dealing with loss and separation from an earlier experience in life. Sometimes when a person experiences a tragic loss it will bring up their previous losses. And if there seems to be difficulty establishing and maintaining intimate relationships and getting on with life goals, it may be due to unfinished business with a previous loss.

UNFINISHED BUSINESS OF LOSS

As we discuss unfinished business, we're referring to unspoken words. These are things that the grieving person did not have an opportunity to say to the loved one, or if he had the opportunity he didn't use it. Some examples are unspoken apology, unspoken forgiveness, and unspoken unresolved anger and conflicts which really belong together because apology and forgiveness have to do with resolving conflict.

Maybe the client didn't say, "I'm sorry, will you forgive me?" or didn't say, "I forgive you," for something, and so that becomes unfinished business. Maybe the client wished that he could have heard the person who died say, "I forgive you," or "I'm sorry for the way I treated you," for the abuse or whatever. But the person died before that conversation could ever be experienced.

It may be that certain issues were avoided and maintained as secrets, and so that becomes unfinished business. As we're talking about these areas of unfinished business I'd like you to think about how they would apply to the client who's loved one is still alive but may have these words waiting to be spoken, and about your own relationships and people in your life that you have unfinished business with.

There may be unspoken affection and caring, not having said, "I love you, I care about you, I'll miss you when you die." Unspoken affection and caring also includes not reminiscing with a loved one about all the good times they had together and all the tough times. This is all unexperienced intimacy.

In some families it's very difficult for people to say, "I love you" to each other. It's something that we have to do regularly for it to be part of us, part of our communication. And if we lapse into not saying it and a person dies, after years of not having said it to him, a person may be left feeling regret and guilt.

To do that with a family member you don't love, what is process? You ask, "What gets in the way of loving him?" Maybe anger about unresolved conflict or abuse, infidelity, or addiction. So there is the need to grieve the loss of closeness and caring. Unspoken anger and the underlying sadness need to be put into words.

There may be unspoken goodbyes, if a person dies and the client didn't have a chance to be with the loved one who may have died suddenly or lived too far away. And so a person is left feeling regret. When there is significant unfinished business, there is complicated grief sometimes. It increases the sadness and the regret and the guilt, so it makes grieving more difficult and intense.

We can also speak of unspoken loss of closeness, which is really to do with unresolved issues, unresolved conflict, never being able to talk to the loved one about the closeness that was missed. And so that becomes unfinished business. If a person can address his unfinished business before the loved one dies, then it can make the grieving much easier.

LETTING GO OF EXPECTATIONS OF PARENTAL CARING

A woman who had been sexually abused went to counselors and therapists, and this always came up: the unfinished business she had with her parents because her mother didn't step in and stop the abuse. She followed through on going and talking to her parents because she felt the counselor wanted her to but it didn't do anything for her.

What was she expecting? She was expecting her parents to start the relationship on a different level perhaps. She may have been expecting to have a caring, understanding, supportive relationship with them. If that was what she expected then its understandable she would say nothing changed. When I suggest a client go talk to parents about unfinished business and unresolved issues, it's very important to make clear to her that she's doing this in order to verbalize the issues for herself, not to change the parents. In fact what she may find is that the parents are not going to change. They're not going to be any different than they have ever been.

And how will that leave the client feeling? Frustrated, empty and sad. The client then is faced with having to grieve the reality that the parents are closed rather than open. That was her report after she went there. It was like she had never left home. Everything was exactly the same. She expressed her issues, and they just went on with life. They didn't show any more understanding or caring. It was just the same. So that is the loss then, the death or loss of the relationship, or maybe of the longing to have that relationship, to have the understanding and the openness, the support, and caring.

So the client goes for the client, to let go of the issues and the expectations of getting lost caring. Facing the grief around the reality of that, is fundamental to her healing, so she can let go of expecting others to give her the caring she needs and to face the reality of needing to give herself what she needs by choosing healthy people and by relating to herself and others in healthy ways.

PROTECTION BLOCK

The reason people don't address unfinished business is because of a protection block, which is precisely the same thing the person does to himself around his own pain. The individual who has come through painful life experiences may protect himself from the pain by using denial and a variety of other defenses that we have discussed.

A person doesn't face family members and significant others with unfinished business maybe because of the protection block which is made up of the fear and the guilt: there is the fear of hurting, and the fear of being hurt. If I bring this issue up, if I mention this, I'm going to cause my dying loved one more suffering. It's going to upset my loved one, or from the perspective of the dying person, if I tell my family members that I'm dying it's just going to make them hurt more so I won't tell them, to make it easier for them.

In reality it makes things much more difficult not to tell them. But there's a protection block because of the fear of hurting or being hurt. I won't go to my father because I'm afraid if I do he'll just reject me again, and he'll tell me not to talk like that or not to bring that up now after all these years. There's that fear and that guilt, the fear that if I say something and it hurts the other person, they will be hurt in some way, and then I'll feel guilty about what I said. I'll regret it and so I'm not going to say it in the first place.

GRIEVING THE LOSS OF PARENTAL CARING

Ultimately it's finally coming to terms with the loss of the closeness. There never will be a relationship with that person, and pursuing anything is futile. So if you go to your father to tell him how you feel, your purpose in doing it would be to take care of yourself, to get that stuff from the inside of you to the outside so that you can say, I've said what I needed to say and he did what he did. He did what he had to do, or what he chose to do, and I did what I had to do for myself.

So that's an acceptance. It may involve another level of grieving when you are faced with the reality he's not going to be any different. He's going to be just as rejecting as ever. He may even become more hostile.

What do you do now that you've brought up the unfinished business but there's no positive response? Then there's something else that you have to deal with, isn't there? It's the grief. But you see it's not something new. It's something that has been there all the time. The reality of the closed parent has been your experience all those years. It's not something that just happened now that you've faced him with it. What's happened is maybe you are realizing for the first time what the relationship is really like, so it allows you to get on with grieving the loss of caring. Grieving means feeling the sadness rather than being stuck in the struggle, the anger and conflict, the fight to get the caring. Sadness lets go; anger hangs on.

A client's oldest brother is old enough to be his father, and he always looked at his brother like a father since his dad died several years back. The brother really reminds him of his dad. He would like to have done things with him like he could have done with his dad. But they never really had a chance to be close because he felt that whenever he was with the brother it was exactly like it was with Dad. He doesn't acknowledge the client's presence when he's in the room. So if he went and told his brother that, the client knows what his reaction would be. He says that for him to have to go tell him that and to see his reaction would hurt him even more.

So I say, "Have you ever done it? Have you ever gone and told him and expressed these issues to him?"

He says, "Exactly how I feel? Not really, I guess because of that fear. We only get together maybe once a year. But you know, different times where I have made an attempt to talk to him he just shoos me off like I'm still a little snot-nosed kid."

In preparing a client to actually approach a family member, it's really important to work with him to assess what his style has been in approaching family members. The purpose is to express the issues in a way that does not dump anger but rather expresses the sadness about lost caring. To do this the counselor can use role-play and rehearse ways of expressing issues in a healthy way.

Now if you find that the parent or family member is open to you, then there may be a chance that you can gain something for the rest of your lives together. And if you find that they're just as closed as they ever have been, even if you approach them in a caring, non-dumping way, then that means that it's time to get on with your grieving and let go.

The client fears something terrible is going to happen and find his fear was exaggerated. It's the child in us who is so frightened and so caught up in a protection block that we remain in that child ego state. That's why we recommend that when the client is ready, he approaches the people they have unfinished business with. Doing that allows him to grow up into his adult self.

The child who is either very frightened or very abusive and dumping does the same thing with the parent that the parent perhaps did to the child. The child gets caught up in a fight, or runs away. It's the adult who can face and express the issues in a straightforward caring, sharing kind of way rather than a dumping way. So when a client can do that, he has taken great steps toward growing into his adult self.

Are there ever any families where the child leaves home without unfinished business? Some are pretty close to that but there's no such thing as a perfect family. But if you look at the continuum between the closed, abusive family and the open nurturing family, there are many families on the open, nurturing end. You won't see those families in counseling.

BEHAVIOUR DECISIONS IN GRIEF COUNSELING

Let's look at behaviour decisions in grief counseling. As we said earlier in discussing the counseling process, the behaviour decisions are related directly to the pain. Painful life experiences can result in unhealthy, ineffective behaviours and in destructive attitudes or beliefs about self and others. When a person has strong pain in grief, that pain often results in certain kinds of decisions.

Let's consider the loss of an intimate relationship. Two people have been going together, and they've been very emotionally bonded. They've developed hopes and dreams about their life together, getting married, having a family, and growing old together, and then one person dies, or decides to leave the relationship. The other person may decide never to get too close to anyone again.

I had a client who was in a relationship with a young man and they were going to get married, but she got cold feet and delayed plans. He came over that night at about two o'clock in the morning to try to talk to her, to try to change her mind. He was crossing the street and was struck by a hit-and-run driver and killed. She was left with tremendous guilt. When I saw her in counseling she made comments like, "I don't think I can ever find anyone like him. I don't think I'll get close to anyone again." So she made this very decision: "I will never get too close to anyone."

A woman whose mother died when she was a child got married and had children of her own, but she always maintained a certain distance, an aloofness from them. She made that same kind of decision. If you invest too much, get too close, you may lose again and that will hurt. People often conclude that intimacy isn't worth the risk. Guilt may go with that decision as well. "I will punish myself; I don't deserve to be happy; I don't deserve to be close."

As I'm working with a person to identify his behaviour decisions I may, in a similar way that I give a person a feeling list, give him a list of decisions that people often make. I ask if he can identify what decision he may have made and then invite him to talk about it. These behaviour decisions constitute life patterns attached to a death or to an abusive dysfunctional family of origin experience such as alcoholic parents, abusive parents, or workaholic absent parents. His thinking may be along the lines of: "I will run away, I'll move to another town. I'll move out of this house where this death occurred, where this person who I cared about died. I can't face being around his belongings. Too many memories are here so I'm going to go somewhere else. I'll run away from the pain."

What people don't realize is that the pain isn't in the house, it's up here in the head. You can't run away from that. They can try by using their defenses. They try to run away. They will not get on with their life.

A child who experiences a tragic loss may say, "I won't grow up, I'll just stay stuck where I am." A woman whose father died when she was ten and was 38 when I saw her, was really still a ten year old, emotionally and socially. The man she married was a father for her. She was his child. She couldn't go out of the house because she was agoraphobic. She had a fear of public places. She had to be escorted wherever she went. She never drove a car or worked outside the home. She had a child but the child was more a sibling than a son.

A person may also try to rejoin the lost loved one. What's the ultimate way of rejoining? Suicide. We need to be alert to any possibility that the client is not safe with himself or herself. A less extreme way of rejoining the lost one is to look for him in another person, perhaps someone who resembles the lost person physically or behaviourally.

The client I was speaking of earlier, who found someone who was a father-like figure to her, had made all of these decisions. She found her dead father in the man she married.

She wouldn't grow up and get on with her life. Her father had died of a heart attack the day after he climbed a hill looking for her, and so she felt tremendous guilt because she thought it was her fault for leaving the house. She punished herself by staying stuck in her grief. She wouldn't allow herself to have friends. She wasn't close to anybody except in this safe role as a child of the man she married.

When I said, "I wonder if your father could speak, what would he say to you? Would he want you to make your grief and depression a lifetime monument to him?" Then she was able to let go.

Enshrinement is a way to join a lost person by maintaining the belongings just as they were. I had a client who disassembled his brother's room and reassembled it in his own apartment, and then he would go in there and experience his brother's presence. In his case that kind of enshrinement was due to a very dysfunctional family in which the parents were distant. I don't think he and his brother had a close relationship. When his brother died, it presented him with a very difficult grief experience.

Idealization is when a person tends to see the dead person as perfect, as having no flaws. This may also be a way of protecting against anger or resentment. One way we can begin to help a person remove the idealizing defense is to have him talk about what may have annoyed him just a little bit. Use that same principle of going for the little bits of resentment or irritation, or annoyed feelings. As long as the loved one is up on a pedestal, it becomes a way of hanging on to him.

The client is not ready to say goodbye. And we find that as soon as he are able to achieve a more balanced picture of a loved one, he's able to get on with the grieving. Often it's protection against anger about the death or toward the loved one.

There may be some normal degree of enshrinement or memorializing when someone dies: a tombstone, a benevolent project. Frequently people will maintain the belongings of the loved one. In the near term, they may even keep a place for the loved one at the table. It may become a problem when it continues on for a very long time, for months or years. Keeping the cremated remains may not be a problem by itself, for instance, but the key is if you see other dysfunctional behaviours that indicate the person is stuck and hasn't been able to say good-bye and let go of the loved one.

We also have memorial services and markers where no one is buried, and graves for the unknown soldier and the like. Some people go back again and again to talk to and grieve for the lost person.

The disadvantage of not having a body is that some people find it difficult to accept the reality of the death without it. What I'd like to do now is suggest some therapeutic interventions you may use, especially in relation to the death of a loved one.

INTERVENTIONS TO ENGAGE GRIEF

Here are some therapeutic statements to help the client engage his grief over the death of a loved one:

"What was his name?" or "What favorite name did you call him?"

The name of the loved one is sometimes laden with emotions, so that simply saying his name or nick-name will bring up the sadness of grief.

"Talk about (e.g. Dad). What was he like?"

With that statement we're helping the person to reconstruct images and memories of the person. It's a very broad open-ended intervention.

"Tell me about the good times you had together."

When a person responds to that he is coming up with memories, pictures in the mind about things that happened. As he begins to talk about the good times, he may feel the loss of the good times. He may begin to feel sad because as he begins to talk about the good times, he realizes that the good times are gone. There won't be any more good times. So sadness often comes up. Or conversely, he may realize there were no good times, and that brings up sadness.

"What didn't you like about him even a little bit," is what I may say if a person is idealizing.

Another way to work with idealizing is to exaggerate the idealization by saying, "So your father was absolutely flawless and perfect. Is that what you're saying? Never said an unkind word, never offended anyone?" Idealizing is sometimes a protection or denial of the loss of caring.

"Talk about the illness."

The illness may have been a very difficult period of time, with a lot of suffering. A person may have a lot of feelings recalling that, a lot of mental images and memories about the suffering person. Some people are dying, waiting for death, for years. There may be a feeling of relief when they do die, and maybe there are guilt feelings about feeling relief.

"How did he die?"

This may get into the area of things that the person would prefer not to mention, like suicide or driving drunk. The fact that the person may have committed suicide may have been glossed over or covered up in some way. But as the client describes how the loved one died, you may as a counselor wonder if this was a suicide. You may say, "Have you ever thought that maybe he committed suicide?" Mentioning the unmentionable is often important in order to free up areas of grief, or you may say, "I wonder if he was drinking that night when he died." The client may not have mentioned it, but you may suspect it.

Would you use the word suicide, or would you ask if the dead person perhaps harmed himself? In either case you are helping the client face the unmentionable.

Next I may have the client talk about what it was like being there when the loved one died.
"Were you with him when he died? What was it like?"
Have the client describe those last moments. That's going to be emotional and may facilitate the grieving. There will be again mental images, memories that come up.

Every once in a while as a person is talking and answering our questions, we need to be saying things like, "What are you feeling inside right now as you're talking?" Reach for those feelings periodically. A person can get into just story-telling. Grief counseling is not just about relating experiences. It's about experiencing the feelings of grief that go with those experiences.
If the client wasn't at the deathbed, you may ask, "How did you hear about the death?" This brings up memories about the time and the place that they heard the news of the death.
You've heard me refer to these mental images and memories that come up. Those are inevitable and we can use them therapeutically by tapping into them. You can say, "I wonder if you can see them in your mind as you're talking about them. Tell me what's happening." As I go for the mental image, I use the present tense. "Tell me what you see in your mind right now. What's happening?" and, "What else is happening?"
I had a client who didn't really grieve over her husband's death until I had her recount in detail the last moments of being with him in the hospital room. He died of cancer, and I said, "Tell me who is in the room with you. Is it just you and your husband? Describe the furniture in the room. And tell me what's

happening during the last hour that you're with him. Are there doctors and nurses coming in and out?" She began to relate those movements and images of the last moments, and she went into a sort of trance state. I find that when I have the client use the present tense it's as if they're put back into that time and they relive it. As she began to describe every detail, she finally came to his last breath. As soon as she mentioned that, is when she broke down and cried.

That was the breakthrough for her. Up until that time she had a lot of feeling, but it was almost all anger directed at doctors and nurses. She couldn't get to the sadness until that point.

"What was the funeral and burial like for you?"

Have the client discuss that and describe that, and again have him describe the mental images that come up around that. And when a person cries we need to say, "Just let yourself feel that. It's okay to cry, just let it out. It takes courage to face the pain." Talking about the loss of hopes and dreams helps to get at the anger of feeling cheated.

"What are some why questions?"

Have the client come up with some why questions. Why him, why God and so on. Why did God let this happen? That helps him engage the anger.

WORKING WITH BEHAVIOUR DECISIONS

Now to explore the behaviour decisions and life patterns proceeding from a loss, we can say, "How has your life been affected by his death?"

A person may say in response to that, "Well, I haven't felt like going anywhere. I don't care to visit friends like I used to." What they're telling us is they've made a decision not to get close to others right now. And we can say it in another way: "If he had lived, how do you think your life would be different?" You're asking the same thing but in reverse. She may say, "We would be having a good time visiting and traveling." What she's telling you is she would be getting on with her life. She's saying she made a decision not to get on with her life. I would reflect that back to her.

What if it's just the opposite? What if she said her life would be miserable because he treated her badly? That points to a loss of caring and closeness before the death. It may be that there are feelings of relief around the death that she feels guilty about, so you could explore that.

WORKING WITH UNFINISHED BUSINESS

To explore unfinished business we could say, "What do you wish you had said to him before he died?" or simply, "What was left unsaid or unfinished? What things do you wish you had said but didn't get a chance to?"

And then you may give the client a list of possible unfinished business by saying, "Sometimes people don't get a chance to say I'm sorry or I forgive you, or I love you."

It could also be that he didn't get a chance to talk about the coming death to the loved one. He didn't take the opportunity to reminisce about the good times. "I wonder if you're aware of what you may have wished you could have said, but didn't. I wonder if there are some unresolved issues that you wish you could have cleared up." See whether he's able to identify and explore that. Areas of unfinished business often are not acknowledged or identified until the counseling process has continued for some time.

If the client was in denial right up until the time the person died, then he wouldn't have thought of things to say. In exploring the circumstances around the death, you are going to have opportunities to identify the unresolved issues.

THE EMPTY CHAIR TECHNIQUE

Using the empty chair technique, I used to more commonly invite clients to say goodbye to a loved one, but at some point I decided to invite the client to talk to a loved one about saying goodbye rather than to directly say goodbye. I find it has the same effect but is less confrontational and frightening. It still elicits the emptiness. If I feel a client is very stuck in grief I'll say, "I'd like you to try on saying goodbye. See what it feels like." If a person reports difficulty saying goodbye, or says he doesn't want to, I won't pressure him. What I'll say is, "Maybe it's too soon to say goodbye. It's not easy to let go. It's not something you can hurry or rush. It takes time."

I find that when I do that with people and support their resistance, it makes it easier for them to say goodbye and let go. It's one of those paradoxical interventions. I'll say, "Maybe it's important for you to do more grieving," and support an extension of the grieving process.

An example that comes to mind is of parents who wouldn't let go of their son who had been dead for 20 years. Whenever I visited their apartment or house there was this huge picture of him in their den, but no large pictures of anybody else. All I had to do was accidentally say anything about him or mention his name and the mother broke down. It helped her to hear, "Maybe you're not ready to say goodbye yet. Maybe you need to do more grieving. Maybe you're not ready to say let go, and that's okay. It's okay not to let go yet. It's okay not to say goodbye." If you give the client permission to hang on, then he is more likely to let go. You flow with the resistance. You don't confront it. If you try to knock it down, it's only going to make it stronger.

Another thing I find that works to facilitate grieving is to talk about the cemetery. Just say, "Have you been by the cemetery?" That facilitates a lot of grieving. What do people do when they go to the cemetery? Talk to the loved one either out loud or in their mind. They may straighten or clean up the gravesite.

There was a woman who lost her seventeen-year-old son. He committed suicide by hanging himself under the sun deck. She went to the cemetery at least once every single day to seek forgiveness, to express her guilt and sorrow. She felt very much to blame for his death. And she did contribute to it in some very significant ways. She was emotionally abusive, and a very harsh disciplinarian, and it was out of fear for her son and love for him while also following the example of her own disciplinarian father. Helping her let go of the guilt would partly mean to forgive herself and to talk about whether she thinks her son would forgive her if he could speak to her.

So when we use the empty chair, we are actually doing something very similar to what a person does when he goes to the cemetery, but we're using it as a deliberate technique. So I'd like to go through the process and just describe how you would introduce the use of the empty chair. It is a particularly powerful technique for helping a person to address unfinished business.

First of all I won't introduce it until about the third or fourth session because it's very important to have a strong therapeutic alliance first. You need to have developed safety and trust in the relationship because it's usually quite different from what people are use to.

The counselor also has to feel comfortable and confident with the technique. That is true of any technique, but especially of the empty chair. I may introduce it is by saying, "I'd like to suggest an exercise to help you explore your feelings a little bit further. Is that something you would want to do today?" The person will give permission, which is essential, and then I'll get up and bring an empty chair to face him. I'll place my chair to the side, so I can still talk comfortably with the client, but I'm not a part of any conversation the client directs toward the empty chair. Then I'll warm up the client to the exercise a little bit further by having him provide a physical description of the person that the client is going to be addressing: the one who died.

I'll say, "To begin this exercise I would like for you to imagine...." I use the word "imagine," not pretend, because pretend has connotations of a child's game. I'll say, "I'd like for you to imagine that your mother is sitting here right now and to help us to begin to imagine her..." and here I use the word "us" to join the client in imagining, "...I'd like for you to begin to describe what she looks like, how tall is she, is she thin, medium weight, overweight? What colour is her hair? Is she wearing glasses?" And I'm using the present tense. That makes the image more real for the client. "What is she wearing right now? How would you describe the shape of her face? Does she have any jewelry? Is she wearing glasses?"

When I feel I have a clear enough image myself, which is how I assess whether the client is able to imagine the person, I'll say, "I'd like for you to begin to speak to your mother and say anything to her that comes to mind. Anything at all is fine." To the very resistant client I'll say, "Just say something very brief, just a little bit of something." Again it's the concept of saying just a little bit. At first a client may say something to me like, "I don't know what to say." I'll say, "Say that to your mother." That's a way to get a person started.

Once the client gets started he can go from there. I'll say, "Go on with that." If there is any sign of tearing, or emotion, or conspicuous silence, I'll say, "Let yourself feel that right now. Stay with the feeling." Keep in mind the goal is grieving, not just to do the empty chair.

And when a client identifies a feeling, I'll have him report it to the loved one instead of to me. He may report it initially to me, and then I'll say, "Tell your mother about the sadness," or the anger, or whatever it is.

If a person asks a question of a loved one, I'll have him sit in the loved one's chair. I'll say, "I want you to sit in Mom's chair and respond in her characteristic way. Respond the way you think she would." And then when he is finished have him return to his own seat and carry on.

It's especially important to do the reversing when a person says "I'm sorry," because "I'm sorry" implies the need for forgiveness. So if a client says, "I'm sorry for...," then I'll say, "Sit in your mother's chair and respond in her characteristic way to your apology." And I'm going to be listening for whether mother is forgiving or not.

If mother cannot be forgiving, maybe that is mother's characteristic way. The client is faced not only with the death as a loss, but the lifetime relationship as a loss because if mother was unforgiving in life, that indicates the loss of caring and closeness. So there's a double level of loss that the client needs to come to terms with. Then I'll say, "What are some areas of unfinished business?" I explore that and continue to help the client to put that into words.

resistance to the empty chair

Above I said at first a client may say something like, "I don't know what to say." I'll say, "Say that to your mother." That's a way to get a person started.

Another approach is to reflect the client: "Yes maybe it seems ridiculous to talk to an empty chair. It's not something you do every day. Try it anyway and see what happens." This approach validates the resistance yet refuses to give it power.

Another more effective approach is to say: "Talk to me about your mother. What was she like?" The idea here is to engage the client in talking briefly about the person in the empty chair. Then simply wave your hand toward the empty chair and say, "Tell that to your mother."

bringing closure to the empty chair exercise

In closure I'll be saying, "I'd like to bring this to a close in just a few moments. I wonder if there is something that you need or want to say before we close, that you'd regret not saying if we were to close without saying it?" That gives a person one final opportunity to say something else. Then we close. I'll say, "Perhaps we can close the exercise right now," and then I'll turn to the client and say, "What has it been like doing this?"

This last question is a review or debriefing of what the exercise was like, and sorting out feelings and insights and whatever came out of that exercise.

forgiveness, idealizing, protection

What happens when someone asks for forgiveness, and when he moves to the empty chair and responds as the loved one, the loved one doesn't forgive him? It means that the client is left with the guilt. He is not going to get forgiveness from the other person. He can give himself forgiveness, but the question is whether hanging on to the guilt means he is hanging on to this person. What punishment does he feel he deserves? Not what punishment does he really deserve but what punishment does he think he deserves? Is he going to give himself a life sentence? Because ultimately it comes down to whether the person can forgive himself.

What about the person who idealizes the parent and in assuming the role of parent in a role reversal portrays the parent responding unrealistically and forgiving the client without dealing with the reality of the situation?

Well, if the client has idealized the parent, the parent has probably been a person who is easy to idealize. In other words, he probably was a forgiving person, but also had other flaws that the client has overlooked or has glossed over. The client is ignoring those flaws as a way of hanging on.

I may say, "What may have annoyed you slightly?" Or I may use exaggeration by saying, "So he was perfect and never made a mistake." The client will most likely retract the idealistic claims. Once the client identifies anything as annoying or less than perfect, I will focus on that and explore the client's feelings about it.

It may also be the case that the client feels sad for the parent's hard life and wants to protect them from further pain or from the client's anger and disapproval. With idealizing we ask the client to talk about minor weaknesses of this parent, how the parent fell short of the caring nurturing parent the client needed. In the case of the abused parent, ask the client to talk about what he or she missed out on: "You feel sad for your parent. What do you feel for yourself?" and, "What did you miss out on because your kind mother was too passive and didn't protect you from dad?" and, "What emotions come up as you talk about that?"

PACE OF THE SESSION

The pace of the session is slow if the client is working, healing, and grieving. You can slow the pace by talking slowly or by asking the client to take some time in silence and just feel: "Take a moment and just feel that now."

A client may want to talk fast and use a lot of words as a defense. Silence often brings up the pain while a stream of words talks it away. You can say, "Sometimes people want to talk away the pain. What are you feeling as you talk? Take a moment of silence and get in touch with that."

OPENING THE SESSION

I want to point out a couple of things about the opening of the grief counseling session and the over-all process that distinguishes it from other types of counseling sessions. If we're working with somebody who has identified some type of a goal or problem that he is experiencing now in his life, we would be working from present experience back to the original loss or conflict, working through painful emotions, then bringing it back up again to help a person gain insight into patterns of behaviour that spring from the original loss. In other words, if the client starts with a presentation of current struggles or symptoms behaviours and problems, you would go from the present to the past, then to the present again.

When you are working with grief, the client is going to identify the loss, and you are going to move from the experience of the loss forward in time to the present as you explore the affects of the loss and grief on the life of the client.

Here are some sample statements in a kind of order:

1. Identify the loss: "What loss do you want to talk about?"
2. Identify emotions: "What emotions come up as you talk about that right now?"
3. Engaging the emotion: "Let yourself feel that right now."
4. Validating the emotion: "Is it OK to feel that?"
5. Patterns of emotional coping: "What have you done with the emotion (fear, anger, guilt, sadness, emptiness, low self-worth, despair)?"
6. Patterns of behaviour: "How has it affected your life?"

In a practice session on grief counseling, begin by asking your client what loss he or she would like to talk about today, and then proceed by using the interventions we've been talking about, especially helping the person identify and experience any emotions related to the loss. Then you could explore how that loss or those emotions have affected her life. You can also explore some behaviour decisions or patterns that come from the loss.

DEMONSTRATION OF GRIEF COUNSELING

The following is a brief excerpt of a session focusing mostly on changing behaviour patterns that resulted from a loss.

Counselor: Talk about a major or minor loss that you have thought about.
Client: My father's death when I was ten.
Counselor: Say a little more about what happened.
Client: I didn't know him very well.
Counselor: What emotions come up as you're talking? A little sadness, emptiness, some other feeling?
Client: A little sadness I guess.
Counselor: What is the sadness about?
Client: Not having him to do things with. There was just mom and me when I was growing up. Other kids had their fathers to go camping with, play sports, and just to be around.
Counselor: So maybe you feel a little cheated because your dad wasn't there for you when you needed him growing up?
Client: Yes.
Counselor: Is it OK to feel cheated?
Client: Yes I guess so, but it wasn't his fault.
Counselor: It's no ones fault that he died, and it's normal to feel cheated about what you missed out on. How do you imagine your life may be different today, if dad had lived and done things with you as a child?
Client: Maybe I would be more outgoing and sociable, not as withdrawn; maybe more confident.
Counselor: So if dad had been there for you growing up, you would be more courageous and more supportive of yourself in life situations.
Client: Yes, I think so.
Counselor: So I wonder if hanging on to being withdrawn may be a way of hanging on to the childhood loss of father.
Client: I never thought of it that way before.
Counselor: If you can imagine that you had an encouraging father, you can bring the feeling of confidence forward to life situations today and be the encouraging father for yourself that you needed.
Client: How?

Counselor: What kinds of things did you need to hear from father if he had lived?
Client: "I believe in you. Take a risk. Have courage. Don't be afraid. Do it anyway. You can do it."
Counselor: What's it like hearing yourself say those things?
Client: It feels good. Like I'm talking myself into being more confident, not so shy.
Counselor: Yes, you're giving yourself the encouragement and support you needed from dad. That's sounds like an important step and significant progress.

review of a grief counseling practice session

The following is a brief discussion of what counselors in training thought their counselors did that was most helpful to them as clients in their practice sessions.

1. I thought John had a lot of empathy and let me say what I wanted to say. I felt he didn't push me in any way. And he made me really feel good. He never suggested anything that I may have not been feeling. He just let me flow with it and I felt it was really good.
2. I liked hearing the reflective statements, just to make sure that what I was saying was on track and also that I was clear in what I was saying.
3. My counselor was very supportive. Also, I like to wander off the topic sometimes, but it's more satisfying when you feel like something is being done. My counselor looked for links between topics that I was talking about.
4. I felt very comfortable with Mike, and that was very helpful. It was the warmth or the gentleness, his non-threatening affect. And it was reassuring to hear him say things like, "Are you comfortable with this, do you want to carry this on?"

Instructor comment: When you ask a client if he is comfortable, that may be a way of checking out whether he feels safe enough. In fact your client may not feel comfortable at all and it may not be to his benefit to feel comfortable. So the word safe may be more accurate. "Do you feel safe enough?" or "What's this like doing this so far today?" Let your client respond to that.

5. As a counselor I discovered I was still over-directing. So when I was counseling John, I ended up telling him what to do. It's helpful to get this feedback. I'm not making them safe. I understand the discomfort that can come through the growth, but I have to make it safe for the client.

6. I found that the issue I thought was the important one turned out to be a cover for something else. It started out as loss of childhood and really it was why did I lose that childhood, and who was the person responsible, and that really is the loss. I'd always dealt with it intellectually before but focusing on the visual images helped my emotions to start coming out. If a child has lost his childhood, there is an adult who is responsible for that. Adults are responsible for children.

7. I had the same experience. The original loss we were going to talk about became something much more important. It was interesting what they'll get around to if you just hang in there with them, and give them safety.

8. I felt with John that we explored every feeling. He'd ask something like, "Did it make you feel angry?" We got right through it. I was really impressed.

Instructor comment: One comment about the phrasing of an intervention. Rather than say, "How did that make you feel?" we need to say, "What are you left feeling?" or "What emotion comes up inside?" When we imply or say, "How does that *make* you feel?" something unhealthy is supported. We are saying somebody else or circumstance controls the emotions; the client is powerless, a victim of circumstances or of others.

Index

addiction as loss, 12, 30
bankruptcy as loss, 12, 13
behavior decisions of, 15, 35, 36
  working with, 41, 49
birth as loss, 8, 9
  of sibling, 11
death of loved one, 7, 13, 16, 21, 22, 25, 27, 29, 30, 32, 36, 37, 38, 39, 40, 42, 43, 45, 47
developmental change as loss, 10
divorce as loss, 11, 24
demonstration of session, 49-51
empty chair, 43-47
  closure of, 46
  introducing, 44-45
  resistance to, 46
  saying goodbye, 15, 25, 29, 30
  unfinished business, 43, 46, 47
  warm-up, 44
engaging grieving, 17, 28, 38, 41, 49
enshrinement, 37
exaggeration, use of, 22, 23, 39, 47
forgiveness, 29, 42, 44, 46, 47
goals of counseling, 7, 14, 15, 16, 45

goodbye, saying, 15, 25, 30, 37, 43
grief, painful emotions of, 7, 13, 14, 15, 16, 17, 23, 25, 28, 48
  interventions for, 16
    anger, 13, 14, 18, 19, 20, 21, 22, 23, 24, 25, 29, 30, 33, 34, 37, 41, 48
    despair, 13, 15, 25, 28, 49
    emptiness, 10, 11, 13, 18, 19, 24, 25, 27, 31, 43
    fear, 13, 14, 15, 17-18, 19, 25, 28, 32, 33, 34, 36, 44
    guilt, 13, 14, 18, 19, 22, 23, 24, 27, 30, 32, 35, 37, 39, 42, 44, 47
    low self-worth, 13, 27-28, 49
    sadness, 13, 16, 18, 20-21, 24, 25, 30, 31, 33, 34, 38, 39, 41, 48, 50
hanging on, letting go, 23-24, 26, 29, 33, 37, 43, 47, 50
idealization, 37, 39, 47, 48
keywords, use of, 21
length of grief, 26
life patterns, from loss, 36, 41, 48, 49
loss,
  hidden, 26
  multiple, 14

loss (cont'd)
  prior, affecting, 26, 28-29
  types of, 7, 8-13, 14, 26
  marriage as, 9, 11, 26, 27
mental images, use of,
  21, 38, 39, 40, 41, 45, 52
minimizing, use of, 19, 22
opening the session, 48-49
pace of session, 18, 48-49

parental caring,
  grieving, 31, 32-34
  loss of, 8, 16, 20, 37, 48
practice session, 49-52
protection block, 32, 34, 37,
  39, 47-48
unfinished business, 7, 15, 32
  working with, 29-30, 31,
  33, 34, 42-46

About the Author

Daniel Keeran, born in 1947 in Marion, Ohio, lives in Victoria, Canada, and Kailua Kona, Hawaii. After completing an MSW degree at the University of Louisville, Kent School of Social Work in 1977, the author gained clinical experience in counseling and psychotherapy in hospital settings and in private practice. With his wife Jennie, he founded the Counselor Training Institute in 1985 expanding to five cities, and in 2005 they began the HomelessPartners.com program designed to connect the public to individual homeless people in shelters. This program is currently operating in over ten US and Canadian cities. He co-founded the national Professional Counselors Association, and he is President of the College and Registry of Mental Health Counseling (www.collegemhc.com).

The author produced a previous volume, entitled *Healing Words,* of the College manual published currently as *Effective Counseling Skills: the practical wording of therapeutic statements and processes.* Two clinical diaries for client use are *The Personal Counseling Journal* and *The Personal Recovery Journal* for the purpose of journaling one's progress in counseling. Other titles are related to philosophy as well as instructional audio material on grief counseling and conflict resolution skills.

Printed in Great Britain
by Amazon